SLADE IN 1971

TONY CHARLES

POUK HILL PRESS

INDEX

BEFORE 1971

Neville John Holder was born in Walsall, Staffordshire. He formed his first beat group at school. They were called The Rockin' Phantoms – later shortened to The Rockin' Phantoms – and soon the name was changed once again to The Memphis Cut-Outs. Their partnering up with the highly-regarded Midlands musician Steve Brett was a step up the ladder and brought in a welcome amount of club work. The group became the new version of his backing band The Mavericks. They would record a series of singles in 1965 on the Columbia label, all of which were credited to Steve Brett.

Donald George Powell and David John Hill (the odd one out of the group, as he was born in Devon) were both members of a local group The Vendors, whose earliest recording career consisted of a 4-song demo acetate recorded at the Domino studios in nearby Albrighton. The group would drop that name and become The N'Betweens. A recording session at Pye Studios in London produced another 4 songs, but Pye didn't sign them. The French label Barclay would release a four track EP, consisting of a further four new cover versions.

Both groups did stints in the clubs in Germany, where bands had to play long and exhausting sessions and try not to repeat themselves too much.

James Whild Lea was a precocious schoolboy talent and he played violin in the Staffordshire Youth Orchestra. His foray into playing with beat groups began at the age of 14, when he joined Nick And The Axemen – a group comprised of school friends. He spotted an advert in the local paper looking for a new bassist for The N'Betweens and would join them, along with the other new member, Noddy Holder. Jim's mother was not amused, as she thought he was going to become a highly regarded, famous, highbrow classical musician.

The new 1966 version of The N'Betweens were initially a five-piece group, until singer Johnny Howells decided, after a few months, that they were moving too far away from playing the blues style music that he loved and was known for. He worked his notice and the other four rehearsed a new set of songs and changed direction toward a more pop-rock oriented setlist. They would gather in the local record shop, The Diskery and go through the latest American import singles, snapping up the ones that they thought would suit them.

The four man N'Betweens released a cover version of The Young Rascals You Better Run on the Columbia label in November 1966, which was produced by American 'freak' Kim Fowley. Their first American release was a promo-only single featuring a cover of Otis Redding's song Security. Fowley went back to the USA and the group carried on as usual.

A trial session at Abbey Road for EMI in April 1967 produced just one song, Delighted To See You, originally recorded by The Honeybus. EMI did not choose to sign the band and producer Norman Smith allegedly didn't think that much of them.

In 1968, the band were still busy in pubs and clubs, and the offer of a residency a club in The Bahamas came through their booking agent. The group went there and played for a few months, backing strippers and fire-eaters, as well as playing their own show. They were suddenly presented with a huge bill for their living expenses, as the club had changed hands. They probably didn't have a copy of the contract that said the club owner would cover them. Their agents didn't help at all. The group worked off their debt and escaped home, doing a bunk when the club was closed for a week for a refurbishment. They changed booking agents upon their return.

Through their new agent's connections, they secured a new recording deal with Fontana and changed their name to Ambrose Slade on January 1st 1969. In May 1969 they released their debut single Genesis / Roach Daddy. It was followed later on in that month by their Beginnings album, which consisted mainly of a selection of the eclectic cover versions that they played in their live show.

The group were playing at the Tiles nightclub in London, when they were discovered by Chas Chandler, formerly the bass guitarist with The Animals. He had previously managed the guitar megastar Jimi Hendrix and was looking for a promising new group to manage. Of course Ambrose Slade blew him away.

With their name now shortened to Slade, a further Fontana single, Wild Winds Are Blowing / One Way Hotel, was produced by Chas Chandler. They were confusingly called 'The Slade' on the single label. They would perform the A-side on TV, along with Martha My Dear (originally by The Beatles) from Beginnings.

4

It would not be difficult to pick the band out from the rest of the crowd, as they had adopted the skinhead style, on the advice of their publicist, Keith Altham. The group went along with the haircuts, though not all of them were happy about the plan.

They were becoming well known, due to the image change. It gained the group a lot of press, but it was not all positive. The group looked too scary for some venues, as skinheads were usually associated with violence and trouble. The look brought them unwelcome attention and occasion conflict.

They all started to grow their hair again and were relieved to be able to do so. 1970 saw the band put out two more singles and the Play It Loud album. They played one-nighters in clubs at a bewildering and back-breaking rate.

They all still lived at home with their long suffering parents who would be woken in the middle of the night by one or the other of the group banging into things, carrying guitar cases in the dark.

And so to 1971…

JANUARY 1971

Friday 1st - Civic Hall. North Street, Wolverhampton
Raymond Froggatt / Ashley / Abel Fletcher

Wolves Supporters Club

Annual New Year's Ball

TONIGHT (FRIDAY),
JAN. 1st, 1971
CIVIC & WULFRUN HALLS

presenting

RAYMOND FROGGATT
SLADE : ASHLEY
ABEL FLETCHER
Plus DISCO
with
The General
Clint Cristian

Dancing 8.0 p.m. to 2.0 a.m.

LICENSED BAR 8.0 P.M.
TO 1.0 A.M.

Tickets 10/6 available now
from Civic Hall, Wolverhampton

LATE TRANSPORT AVAILABLE

Monday 11th - BBC recording studio. Delaware Road, Maida Vale, London
Recording Mike Harding Show

The historic Maida Vale BBC studios.

Tuesday 12th – The previous day's recording for the Mike Harding Show is broadcast, BBC Radio1.

Wednesday 13th - Caerlon College. College Road, Newport

7

Thursday 14th - Red Dragon, St Athans, Wales

Saturday 16th - University. Richmond Road, Bradford

Monday 18th - Top Rank Club. Queen Street, Cardiff
(College of Education Coming Up Ball). Support: McArthur Park / Cactus Jam

at Doncaster Top Rank on January 29. ● Tremeloes at Cardiff Tito's tomorrow (Saturday). ● Frankie Vaughan commences two-week cabaret season at Batley Variety Club on January 24. ● White Plains doubling Doncaster Ki-Ki and Barnsley Ba-Ba for three days this weekend (15-17). ● Steamhammer at Derby Clouds (January 21) and Welwyn Garden City Community Centre (22). ● Slade at Bradford University (tomorrow, Saturday) and Barry College of Education (next Monday). ● Brett Marvin & the Thunderbolts at Leeds Polytechnic (tonight, Friday) and Colchester Essex University (Saturday). ● Syd Lawrence Orchestra at Bradford Festival on March 13. TONIGHT (Friday), Osibisa at Wimbledon Hobbit's Garden, Juicy Lucy at London Queen Mary College, Black Widow and Demon Fuzz at Welwyn Garden City Community Centre, Steeleye Span at Hampstead Country Club, Every Which Way at Uxbridge Brunel University, Swegas at London Temple and Stray at London Marquee.

DANCES

CARDIFF COLLEGE OF EDUCATION

COMING UP BALL

MONDAY 18th JAN.

with **SLADE**
McARTHUR PARK
CACTUS JAM
and D.J.

CARDIFF TOP RANK SUITE

BARRY COLLEGE OF FURTHER EDUCATION STUDENTS' UNION
presents
DANCING TO GROUNDHOGS, BLONDE ON, BLONDE & DISCOTHEQUE
At BARRY MEMORIAL HALL
Tuesday, 19th Jan.
7.30 to 11.30. Doors close 9.30
Tickets in advance 15/- from College.

Tuesday 19th - Sounds of the 70's with Mike Harding - BBC Radio 1
Also featuring War Horse.

Saturday 23rd - University College, Dumfries Place, Cardiff, Wales.

Cardiff University SU.

Sunday 31st - Lyceum. Wellington Street, London
With Argent – Slade - Roy Young Band – Barclay James Harvest.

SUNDAY LYCEUM
LYCEUM STRAND WC2

SUNDAY JANUARY 31st

ARGENT
SLADE
BARCLAY JAMES HARVEST
ROY YOUNG BAND

—— 6.30 - 11.30 ——

ANDY DUNKLEY adm 9/- PROTEUS LIGHTS

The Lyceum, London

FEBRUARY 1971

Friday 5th - Tricorn Club. Tricorn Centre , Market Way , Portsmouth

TRICORN CLUB
Tricorn Centre,
Market Way, Portsmouth.
Booked through
M.M.F. GOSPORT 81867

Thurs, Feb. 4
FREE FERRY
Fri, Feb. 5
SLADE
Sat, Feb. 6
THUNDERCLAP NEWMAN
Sun, Feb. 7
OFF THE RECORD
with D.J. Pete Cross
Mon, Feb. 8
CHANCERY LANE
Tues, Feb. 9
TRAPEZE
+ Pete Drummond
+ **SWEET THUNDER**

Saturday 6th - University of Southampton, University Road, Southampton
Keef Hartley / Slade / Tir Na Nog

High Tide, Mr. Bizarre, Graphite; Southampton D-Rag, Emerson Lake and Palmer. Fri. Feb. 5, Luton Col. of Tech., Kinks; Lanchester, Elton John, Caravan, Skid Row; Hendon Coll. Tech., Mick Abrahams, Gringo; Southampton, Michael Chapman; Sunderland Poly, Love Affair; East Anglia, Soft Machine. Sat. Feb. 6, Leeds, Elton John; UCL, Soft Robert and itinerant musicians; Imperial College, Bronco, Quiver; Sheffield, Airforce; Lanchester, Ralph McTell, Strawbs, Mr. Fox; Bradford, Man, Principal Edwards; Liverpool Poly, Free; Southampton, Keef Hartley, Slade, Tir Na Nog; Univ. of Surrey, Root and Jenny Jackson, Herbie Goins; Hall Green Tech.; Brim, Tea and Symphony; Durham, Skin Alloy, Evil Past. Sun. Feb. 7, Lanchester, John Williams, Ronnie Scott, Nucleus.

Southampton University

13

Monday 8th - Top Rank. Queen Street, Cardiff

Tuesday 9th – The Showboat. Above Castleton Walk Arcade, Mumbles, Swansea

The Showboat was above a cinema (The Regent) which closed down in the early 80's to make way for a shopping arcade. The upstairs area remained as a disco and is now a soft play centre for the grandchildren of those 70's gig-goers.

Tuesday 9th - Sounds of the 70's BBC Radio
Also featuring Walrus

Friday 12th -Scotland

Saturday 13th - Grand Hall. Green Street, Kilmarnock
Support: Northwind

GRAND HALL DANCING

KILMARNOCK

TOMORROW (SATURDAY)   7.30 p.m. to 11 p.m.

SLADE

and

NORTHWIND

ADMISSION — 8/-

Quite a grand building, so the Grand Hall can be assumed to really be quite grand indeed.

Sunday 14th - Scotland

Friday 19th – Scotland

Saturday 20th - Farx Club. Elm Court Youth Centre, Mutton Lane, Potters Bar
Support: Renia / Crushed Butler

Future members of The Sensational Alex Harvey Band were not far away, supporting a band called
Satisfaction. One has to wonder if they featured the Rolling Stones song in their show. Probably.

Wednesday 24th - California Ballroom. Whipsnade Road, Dunstable

This absolutely fantastic and historically important venue has sadly been long demolished. It hosted a long series of shows by some of what would become the world's top bands.

There were many objections and protests before it was demolished, but it went and all that remains now is a road sign acknowledging that it had once been there.

Thursday 25th February - Alsager College. Crewe Road, Alsager, Cheshire.

Friday 26th - Town Hall. High Street, Uttoxeter

A quiet little town, but maybe not that night...

CAVENDISH SUITE

VICTORIA HOTEL, WOLVERHAMPTON (ENTRANCE BERRY ST.)

OVER 18's DISCO CLUB, SUNDAY

FINALS MISS HOT PANTS OF WOLVERHAMPTON COMPETITION

TONIGHT IS YOUR LAST CHANCE TO ENTER !

Your Hosts: Mickey Dunne, Clint Cristian and Big John

8.0 p.m. to 12.0 midnight Free Membership No Unorthodox Dress Ties Must Be Worn Doors Close 10.15 p.m.

Queen Mary Ballroom

DUDLEY ZOO GROUNDS

TONIGHT (SATURDAY)

BARMY BARRY presents

SLADE   SLADE   SLADE

SUNDAY CLUB

CARL DENE ROADSHOW

THE CONNAUGHT HOTEL

TETTENHALL ROAD, WOLVERHAMPTON

Tonight (Saturday)

Dance to be held in the CAVENDISH SUITE
Berry Street, W'ton, Rear of Victoria Hotel

JUG : JUG : JUG

Sunday Special Here at The Connaught:

IDLE RACE : IDLE RACE

PLUS, OF COURSE, CRUSOE PLUS ALAN S.

MARCH 1971

Tuesday 2nd - St Giles Youth Club. Walsall Street, Willenhall
(Due to demand, Slade would be booked to play two sessions that evening)

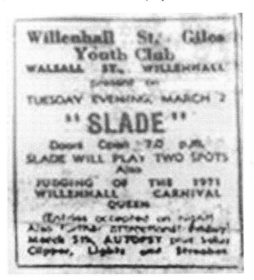

The Youth Club is the white building on the right

Saturday 6th - Polytechnic, Wolverhampton.

SLADE : SLADE
PLUS DISCO AND LIGHTS
SATURDAY, MARCH 6th, 8.0 p.m. till midnight. Admission 25p
S.U. POLYTECHNIC
STAFFORD STREET   WOLVERHAMPTON

JOHN SMITH ENTERTAINMENTS AGENCY presents
EMERSON LAKE & PALMER
IN CONCERT
Civic Hall, Wolverhampton
SUNDAY, MARCH 14th, 7.30 p.m.
Tickets £1, 85p, 75p, 65p, 50p from Civic Hall Booking Office.

Wolverhampton Polytechnic

Sunday 7th - Connaught Hotel. Tettenhall Road, Wolverhampton

THE CONNAUGHT HOTEL
TETTENHALL ROAD, WOLVERHAMPTON
Tonight (Saturday)
DICTIONARY OF SOUL
Tomorrow (Sunday)
SLADE : SLADE
Plus · ALAN S. *Plus* CRUSOE

Tuesday 9th - Kings Hall. Kings Avenue, Prestatyn
Support: Gorilla / Smokestack

Friday 12th - Patti Club. Gorse Lane, Swansea.
Support: Fungus

PATTI PAVILION, SWANSEA

TONIGHT

SLADE

AND

FUNGUS

Doors open from 8 p.m. to midnight. Adm. 50p. Bar 8.00 - 11.00

Saturday 13th - Gala Club. St Stephens Road, Norwich.

Thursday 18th - Kinectic Circus. Bull Ring, Birmingham
Atomic Rooster / Slade / Flying Hat Band

KINETIC CIRCUS
BULL RING
BIRMINGHAM
021-643 2137

TONIGHT
at 7.45 p.m.

ATOMIC
ROOSTER
On stage at 9.45 p.m. approximately
PLUS
SLADE
PLUS
FLYING HAT BAND
SOUNDS BY ERSKINE
LIGHTS BY VISIO WORKSHOP
LICENSED BAR

KINETIC CIRCUS
BULL RING, BIRMINGHAM, 021-643 2137
THURS., MARCH 18th, 7.30 p.m.

ATOMIC ROOSTER
plus **SLADE**

LIGHTS BY VISIO-WORKSHOPS
SOUNDS BY ERSKINE

Advance tickets 50p, from: Kinetic Circus (Mayfair); Discely, Birmingham;
Fennells, Coventry; Beatties, Wolverhampton; Turner Records, West Brom-
wich; Taylor & Sons, Walsall; Rentons, Leamington Spa.

Friday 19th - Chez Club. Leytonstone High Road, Leytonstone

Friday 19th - Temple Club. Wardour St, London
Support: Universe / Flying Fortress

Saturday 20th - University Exeter
Support: Alan Bown

> Atomic Rooster at **Brighton** Big
> Apple, 7.30 p.m. **Alan Bown**
> **and Slade at Exeter University,**
> **8 p.m., 60p.** Candy Floss and
> Mode at **Strathclyde** University,
> 9 p.m. 45p.
> Terry Reid and Black Widow
> at **Dagenham** Roundhouse, 7.30
> p.m. Members 70p, guests 80p.
> Onyx at **Plymouth** Tricorn club,
> 8 p.m. 40p. Patto at **Plymouth**
> Van Dike, 8 p.m. 50p.

Exeter University

Friday 26th - Town Hall . High Street, Uttoxeter (Cancelled)
Friday 26th - College of Commerce. Brunswick Avenue, Hull

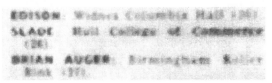

27

APRIL 1971

Friday 2nd - Bishop Lonsdale College. Longsdale Road, Derby

Slade's wild **end** to rag 'rebellion'

AIDED by many pints of brown ale, which weren't really needed, a packed house at Bishop Lonsdale College, Uttoxeter Road, Derby, raved and writhed to the music of Slade, at the End of Rebellion Dance, which brought Rag Week to a close.

It was a return visit for this amazing band who played better than ever.

Their simple, unpretentious, sincere rock, raised the audience to fever pitch, through two ear-blasting sets.

Their ribald comments at themselves and certain members of the audience gave a sort of "village hop" atmosphere, and everyone felt very much at home.

"Knights in White Satin" was slammed out with ease, and Jim Lea on fiddle proved he was just as competent on that as he was on bass.

My favourite number remains "The Dirty Joker,'

which really has got something, even though Dave Hill sounds as if he hasn't. I laughed at his voice the first time, but I will do that no more.

It is weird in the extreme, rather like a musical instrument, but with a higher pitch than any I know.

The second set was an all-out rave, the band playing some great old rock things like "Roll Over Beethoven," with Noddy Holder shouting and screaming the lyrics above Dave's freaky guitar.

In one number he almost took it off while he was still playing and chased Jim and Noddy around the stage with it.

Banned number

Don Powell on drums is the quiet member of the band, but a heavy drummer who is now beating hell out of his kit instead of stroking it. And he sounds much better.

Long gone are the days of their "skinhead" image and aggro. All they want is to see people enjoying themselves. Their happiness is infectious and loud, just like their music.

— *Richard Cox*

Bishop's Lonsdale College.

Saturday 3rd - Castle Hall. West Castle Street, Bridgnorth.

CASTLE   HALL

BRIDGNORTH

TONIGHT   SATURDAY !

Slade   Slade

Plus Sounds by PETE VAN DYKE

LATE DANCING   LICENSED BARS

NEXT SATURDAY : — **BARMY BARRY invites JIGSAW**

The Castle Hall venue

Monday 12th - Windsor Ballroom. Coatham Hotel, Newcommon Road, Redcar

An imposing seafront venue

Friday 16th - Bobby Jones. Burns Statue Square, Ayr, Scotland.
Support: The B J Showband / The Gyro

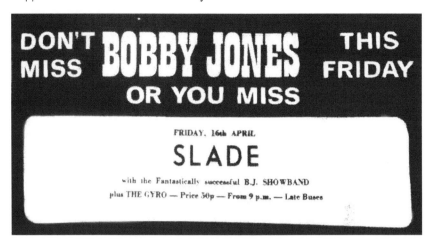

DON'T MISS BOBBY JONES THIS FRIDAY OR YOU MISS

FRIDAY, 16th APRIL

SLADE

with the Fantastically successful B.J. SHOWBAND
plus THE GYRO — Price 50p — From 9 p.m. — Late Buses

Thursday 22nd - Showboat. Newton Road, Mumbles, South Wales.

Friday 23rd I - Trinity College. College Road, Carmarthan, Wales.

Saturday 24th - Glen Ballroom. Waunlanyrafon, Llanelli, Wales.
Support: National Headband

Slade — a maxi single

SLADE, the group who started with but recently abandoned their 'skinhead' image, are the first act to have a maxi-single issued by Polydor.

Set for May 14 release only two of the three titles are named at the moment ... the third is "a surprise for the fans," according to a spokesman.

Titles known so far are "Do You Want Me" and "Get Down And Get With It," both group compositions.

Slade, who are managed by ex-Animal Chas Chandler, have just completed a ten day tour of Scotland and further dates for the band this month are: (April 22) Showboat, Mumbles, South Wales; (23) Trinity College, Carmarthen, Wales; (24) Glen Ballroom, Llanelly, Wales; (28) Newmarket Hall, Bridgwater, Somerset.

Monday 26th April - Cavendish Suite, Wolverhampton.
Support: The Montanas

33

Wednesday 28th April - New Market Hall. Bridgewater Somerset.

MAY 1971

Wednesday 5th - BBC Radio Recording.

Friday 7th - Top Rank. St John Centre, Liverpool.
Support: Bronco – Confucious.

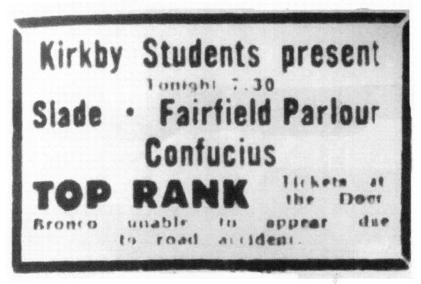

The Top Rank later became the Rotters nightclub and Slade would play there again in 1980.

Thursday 13th - "Sounds of the Seventies"
BBC radio with Stuart Henry also featuring Brett Marvin & the Thunderbolts.

Saturday 15th - Bishops' Barn. Silver Street, Wells

BISHOP'S BARN : WELLS

Saturday, May 1st   **DISCO**   8-11.30 p.m.   25p

Saturday, May 8th
2.30-4 p.m.   **AFTERNOON JUNIOR DISCOTHEQUE!**   10p

✻ **EVENING DISCO**   7.30-11.30 p.m.   25p ✻

Saturday, May 15th   **THE STRANGE BREW MAY RAVE UP!**
with the legendary.

S L A D E   (stars of TV, Radio and Records)

plus, as always

THE GORDON POOLE SUPER SHOW and STRANGE BREW LIGHTS!

It just doesn't look like a rock venue.

36

Friday 21st - Get Down and Get With It released.

SINGLES

Get Down and Get With It/Do You Want Me, Gospel According to Rasputin. Slade (Polydor 2058-112). Slade is a very good group. Unfortunately, they were labelled with the Skinhead tag and now they are trying desperately to lose it. If this record has anything to do with it they will be accepted for what they are — a damn fine rock band. It's real down-to-earth rock 'n' roll in the Little Richard style with a heavy stomping beat. It's a real raver and should be a hit.

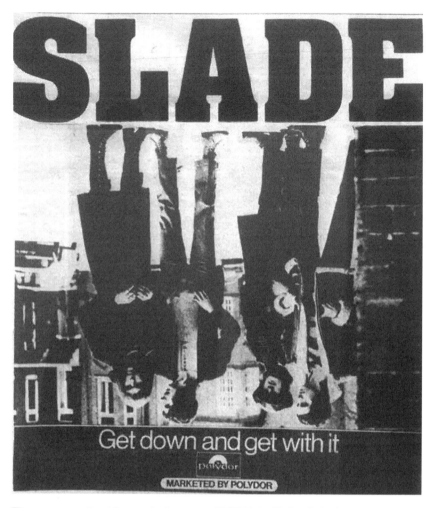

Get down and get with it

MARKETED BY POLYDOR

The song was best known before as a 1967 Little Richard single. It had been a strong stage favourite for the group for quite some time. When the record hit the shops, the A-side was credited to the group and Richard Penniman (Little Richard). None of them had any involvement in the writing of the song, though the Slade version had an extremely different lyric and the arrangement meant it was hardly recognisable as the same song. Whether they were told to correct it, or whether they just did so when they realised their mistake is unclear. Noddy Holder wrote in his autobiography: "The record company sorted out the lawsuit, but we learnt to be more careful in future." The song was written by Bobby Marchan and was a B-side to his Half A Mind single in 1964. The song was actually called Get Down With It.

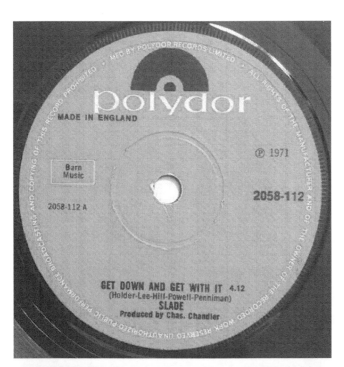

Polydor

MADE IN ENGLAND

℗ 1971

Barn
Music

2058-112 A

2058-112

GET DOWN AND GET WITH IT 4.12
(Holder-Lee-Hill-Powell-Penniman)
SLADE
Produced by Chas. Chandler

Polydor

MADE IN ENGLAND

℗ 1971

Barn
Music

2058-112 B

2058-112

1. **DO YOU WANT ME** 4.30
(Hill-Holder)
2. **GOSPEL ACCORDING TO RASPUTIN** 4.23
(Hill-Holder)
SLADE
Produced by Chas. Chandler

Noddy Holder told Chris Charlesworth: "The first time we heard that was at the Connaught in Wolverhampton and whenever the DJ used to play it, it went down a storm. We started doing it and the skinheads used to love that bit at the finish where you put your hands in the air and take your boots off and all that."

Chas Chandler had told the group that they way they played it live would work well on record and he was right. The single was released in many countries around the world, but it was most successful in the UK, where it reached number 16 and was their first chart success. The group were filmed in a car and walking around a power station in London and the footage was used for a promo film.

The UK B-side featured two new Slade songs, Do You Want me and Gospel According To Rasputin. Do You Want Me had a guitar motif at its centre that was a little similar to that from a song called Offering by Spooky Tooth (from their 1969 album Ceremony), who Slade had supported the previous year.

American record with wrong song-writing credits.

Record Mirror: "It's a scream-up of an adaption of a Little Richard rocker and there's a positive air of desperation as Noddy Holder builds up the excitement"

Roy Carr wrote an article for the New Musical Express:

NEW TO THE CHARTS
THE HAIR-RAISING SAGA OF SLADE.

The continuing saga of Slade would appear to be a case of changing horses in midstream. Originally this pack of Wolverhampton Wanderers were covered in hair and known as Ambrose Slade, a name under which they made a couple of obscure albums and singles for Fontana.

Then around the beginning of 1970, they were denuded of their locks, and their psychedelic apparel replaced by ben Sherman shirts, denims and bovver boots, redubbed SLADE and launched with a hard aggressive record called "The Shape Of Things To Come".

Accompanying the record was a handout, which I found amongst a bunch of old copies of Playboy, a dried up cheese sandwich and subscription to Curious.

It read… "This is the Wolverhampton group who hit the headlines because they realised that long hair had become a lie (oh really), some months later John Winston Lennon reached the same conclusion with the same result.

Slade are symbolic of a new generation who are looking for their own identities – in much the same manner as the mods of yesteryear who found the WHO were wearing their clothes and singing their song – My Generation."

Soon Slade were to known as the bovver boys of pop, but though they projected this hardcase skinhead imagery their music wasn't reggae but heavy rock.

After a while one realised that the group's shiny pates weren't showing through their prickly coiffures. In fact freshly grown locks were hanging over their collars and ear, they had turned full cycle.

Allowing things to die a natural death, they recharged their energies and hit back with a group adaptation of an old Little Richard rocker, "Get Down And Get With It" which has nudged its way into the NME chart this week.

Comprising: Noddy Holder guitar and vocals), Jim Lea (bass, violin and guitar), Dave Hill (lead guitar and saxophone) and Don Powell (drums), Slade have had to contend with lot of questionable publicity which has nothing to do with their music or reality, to their credit they have made the first step to overcome it.

Sunday 23rd - Jungerencentrum. Maastracht, Holland.

Jongerencentrum „Meulewaeg"
Maasbracht
presenteert

TOTAAL PROGRAMMA

m.m.v. de Engelse popformaties

CZAR en SLADE

22 mei   23 mei

Verder o.a. slapstickfilms, bewegingsexpressie, barbecue, creativiteit, Pierre Knoops etc. Entree ƒ 3.50

Friday 28th - Horn Hotel. High Street, Braintree

JUNE 1971

Thursday 10th - Sounds of the 70's with Humble Pie

Friday 11th - Temple Club. Wardour Street, London.
Support: Ginger / Money.

Also on that same week, Brinsley Schwarz, whose singer was Nick Lowe.

Saturday 12th - Park Hall Hotel. Goldthorn Park, Wolverhampton.

CARAVAN in Concert
THIS MONDAY, JUNE 14th, at
Stychfields Hall, Stafford
Doors Open 7.0 p.m. Licensed Bars. Tickets 60p, 70p and 75p from Beatties, Wolverhampton, or available at door on night.

CAMPAIGN FOR SOCIAL JUSTICE IN NORTHERN IRELAND
(Wolverhampton Branch)

GRAND IRISH DANCE
At St. Joseph's Hall, Hickman Avenue, W'ton, on FRIDAY, JUNE 18th, 8.0 p.m. to 1.0 a.m.
Guest of Honour & Speaker: FRANK McMANUS, M.P.
Music: Birmingham Based Irish Show Band, Seamus Dwan's All-Star "Log Cabin Boys." Admission 30p. Licensed Bar. Unity for Justice

The Harrier
POWIS AVENUE   TIPTON

TONIGHT (FRIDAY) We Present, By Public Demand !
HEATHROW
Admission 30p

PARK HALL HOTEL
GOLDTHORN PARK, WOLVERHAMPTON
Tomorrow (Saturday)
SLADE : SLADE
MR. MAX : MR. MAX

Three Men in a Boat
BEECHDALE ESTATE   WALSALL

TONIGHT (FRIDAY)
ERIC AND THE CLUBLANDERS
PLUS SIMON KENT
TOMORROW (SATURDAY) : MAIL PLUS SIMON KENT.

Wednesday 16th - Magdelene College. Magdelene Street, Cambridge

This week's dates

THURSDAY
Alsager College, Stoke: Tir Na Nog
FRIDAY
King's College, Cambridge: Keef Hartley, Arthur Brown, Duster Bennett, Ginger Johnson, Stray and Oberon.
SATURDAY
Alsager College: Da Da
Exeter University: Disco
Bradford University: Roy Young Band
Loughborough University: Rock 'n' Roll All

Stars
St. Mary's College, Twickenham: Paladin
Durham University: Humble Pie and Jericho Jones
MONDAY
Trinity College, Cambridge: Roy Young Band
WEDNESDAY
Brighton College of Education: Fleetwood Mac
Loughborough University: Tekford Hall Disco
Magdalene College, Cambridge: Slade

Friday 18th - Padgate College. Insall Road, Warrington

Thursday 24th - California Ballroom. Whipsnade Road, Dunstable, Luton

JULY 1971

Thursday 1st - Dijkgatbos, Wieringermeer, Holland

1. Hear Me Calling
2. Keep On Rockin'
3. Know Who You Are
4. Sweet Box
5. Get Down With It
6. Born To Be Wild (part)

This show was immortalised with a radio broadcast with certain excerpts later appearing on a bootleg CD.

Friday 2nd - Paradiso Club, Amsterdam Holland

Saturday 3rd - Exit Club, Rotterdam, Holland.

Sunday 4th - Vondelpark, Amsterdam, Holland.

Thursday 8th - Granary Club. Queen Charlotte Street, Bristol
Support: Green Steam.

Events at The Granary
JULY

Thursday 1st : Two firsts for the club tonight with the newly re-organised RENAISSANCE and the well spoken of LEGEND.

Monday 5th : From Israel on a nationwide tour come JERICHO JONES so don't miss them. Also on are the goodly APPLE SNOW.

Tuesday 6th : In respect of many requests, another evening of BLUES with THE TUESDAY BLUES BAND and authentic records.

Thursday 8th : Hot on the heels of their smash single come SLADE plus a fine support band GREEN STEAM.

Monday 12th : The evil Pictish melodies of TEARGAS from Scotland plus the talented TAPESTRY.

Friday 9th - Chez Club. High Road, Leytonstone, London.

The Chez Club venue was in the hall to the rear of the Red Lion pub, which was also a venue.

48

Saturday 10th - The Tropicano . Trinity Street, Fareham.

THIS SATURDAY SEE
SLADE
at
THE TROPICANO
TRINITY STREET,
FAREHAM,
doors open 8.00 p.m.

The name's changed but the building is still there.

Wednesday 14th - Red Lion. High Road, Leytonstone.

Thursday 15th - Regal Hotel, Minehead.
Also Top Of The Pops broadcast for 'Get Down And Get With It'.

Friday 16th - Community Centre - Cwmbran Croesy Ceilog, Wales.

Friday 17th – Slade are featured in a Record Mirror article.

NOW SLADE CAN LAUGH LAST

The boots and braces, brawn and bovver image worked for a time, but now Slade are loath to talk about their Skinhead image. But not because it's something they feel they have left behind, simply that it's not of prime importance.

When we met, the group looked more like the Ambrose Slade of several years ago, who had presented a good, but somewhat uncertain set at Rasputin's.

Softer hair, velvet trousers, leather modern style boots were sprinkled among them, as well as a good measure of confidence.

"The Skinhead scene was something that we got into gradually," Noddy told me. "And it's something we been getting out of gradually. Really we had to get out of it to be accepted by most people."

Despite natural improvements Slade didn't in fact change their original musical ideas, when they adapted their dress. But this was a point they found hard to convince people of.

"We didn't want to change our musical approach", they assured me. "We have always used a variety of material on stage, from Dusty Springfield's 'Going Back' to a heavy Alvin lee number. But people were just anti-Slade.

"When we got on stage they were just astounded. They didn't know what to think.

"Some people get encores automatically, but we had to work for them, and we knew if we got a better response we were going down well because of the music. The trouble was, that we didn't get the type of audience that we wanted at first, but now everybody seems to be booking us, and we get a lot of return bookings."

It was the good stage reaction that made Slade decide to release 'Get Down And Get With It' as a single.

"We brought it out to get it in the charts", said Jimmy. "It was fantastic on stage, we used to use it for our encore number. It's adapted from a Little Richard number, but the other two numbers on the single are our own."

"We use nearly all of our own compositions on stage, but we still do 'Nights In White Satin' with the fiddle!"

Since their chart entry, a stack of demos have arrived for consideration by Slade, including several Randy Newman numbers.

"We've played through all of them", Noddy told me. "But we haven't found anything yet that we really like. We're looking for a follow-up single, but we want something very heavy for that."

"We're also halfway through our second album. We went in the studio with five numbers last week, and came out with three that might be good for singles. We just go along when we've got something good and go in and do it."

Slade now feel that they are breaking ground and entering into more work circuits. But with little help from those who profess to be helpful to people.

"We're not doing any specific circuit", Noddy told me. "Bu since Christmas we've been working more in colleges and universities. We've been wanting to do that for a long time, and some of the places gave us a chance – mainly in the Manchester area. As it turned out we went down very well because we played the heavy stuff. But what annoys me is that it's often the people at the 'heads' places that snub us, and they're supposed to have such an open mind."

"Some of the disc jockeys as well are a bi snobby", added Don. "But we've got round them and we're having the last laugh already! And the places are going to be booking us in the end."

Which sounded like good fighting Skinhead words. "We may well cut our hair off again", laughed Noddy. "In fact in a while we probably will."

In the meantime the group are off to Holland where they are filming their own forty minute television show, and are set to appear at an open air festival.

"In the early days we couldn't see the point of playing at the Rasputin all the time with Chas (Chandler – their manager) bringing people down to see us. We thought it was a drag because we couldn't play as loud as we wanted", Don told me.

"At that time when Chas said he thought we had potential we didn't think we were going to be any different, we were just a group. But Chas has influenced us, and groups we've worked with. Then you tend to look for a sound that is your own."

"Surely it's a sign of success", added Noddy. "When people start copying you."

And has that happened to Slade?

"In a small way it has happened", was the reply. "We find some groups using the same kind of numbers that we do, and using our compositions on stage and on the radio. It makes you feel good.

Val Mabbs

Tuesday 20th - Bumbers Club. Coventry Street, London
/ Radio Luxembourg Personal Appearance.

Wednesday 21st - Rex Ballroom. York Road, Bognor Regis

MELODY MAKER, July 24, 1971—Page 31

marquee

90 Wardour St., W.1 — 01-437 2375

Thurs., 22nd July (7.30-11.0)

★ **SLADE**

★ Plus supporting attraction

Fri. 23rd July (7.30-11.0)

★ **STUD** plus FRUPP

Sat., 24th July (7.30-midnight)
DISCO/DANCE NIGHT

★ **D.J. JOHN ANTHONY**
From America

★ **EARLINE BENTLEY**

Sun., 25th July (7.00-11.00)

★ **CHANGO**
★ **DIABOLUS**

D.J. Jerry Floyd

Mon., 26th July (7.30-11.0)

★ **ASSAGAI**

★ Plus Guest Group

Tues., 27th July (7.30-11.0)

★ **TERRY REID**

★ **GNIDROLOG**

Wed., 28th July (7.30-11.30)
MIDWEEK DISCO/DANCE NIGHT
Pearl Connor Presents

★ **HAPPY DAYS**

Thurs., 29th July (7.30-11.0)
GLEN CORNICK'S

★ **WILD TURKEY**

THE CASTLE. TOOTING BROADWAY
1 MINUTE TOOTING TUBE

Wednesday, July 28

MICK ABRAHAM

HEADLIGHTS   DJ PETE PARFITT

VILLAGE   Roundhouse, Lodge Ave., Dagenham

Saturday, 24th July

RORY GALLAGHER!

Next week Sam Apple Pie

Licensed Bars   Doors open 7.30   Light show

Friday 23rd - Paget Rooms. Victoria Road, Penarth
Support: Karakorum

PAGET ROOMS
PENARTH
FRIDAY, 23rd JULY, '71
7.30 - Midnight
SLADE
KARAKORUM
Lights by Pagic Patch
Admission 50p

WANTED

EXPERIENCED Drummer required for top Cardiff Club. Guaranteed five nights a week. Must be good reader. — Ring Hengoed 2378.

...Slade fans riot at club

The presence of Slade caused a near riot in Scotland last week, when over 30 fans were arrested outside the Cosmos Youth Centre in St Andrews. Over 500 fans had crossed the Tay Bridge from Dundee to attend Slade's performance, only to find the doors of the centre closed and a "members only" notice posted.

Police herded most of the youngsters back over the bridge, but some were charged with obstruction in the process. Meanwhile, Slade played to 1,000 inside the club.

SLADE FANS 'GET DOWN' TO A RIOT

SLADE fans in Scotland took the advice of the group's hit single, 'Get Down And Get With It', a little too literally last week.

Over 500 of them, locked out of a Slade gig, caused a near-riot, quelled only by police who arrested over 30 protesting fans.

While Slade played to 1,000 fans inside the Cosmos Youth Centre, St Andrews, 500 fans from nearby Dundee crossed the Tay bridge to find the club doors closed and a "Members Only" notice outside.

Police were called in when the fans refused to disperse and arrests were made for obstruction.

Forthcoming Slade gigs are (August 6) Blackwood Institute, Blackwood, Monmouthshire, (7) Gwyn Hall, Neath, Glamorgan, (9) Cooks Ferry Inn, Edmonton, (11) Ballerina Ballroom, Nairn, Scotland.

Yes — a tour and album

DATES have been set for the Yes tour of the UK in October and an album will be released to coincide with it.

The album is titled 'Fragile' and dates so far set are, De Montford Hall, Leicester (September 30), Manchester Free Trade Hall (October 1), Albert Hall, Nottingham (2), Aberdeen (7), London Festival Hall (8), Edinburgh Empire Hall (9), Caird Hall Dundee (10), Colston Hall, Bristol (12), City Hall, Sheffield (13), City Hall, Southampton (14) and ABC Stockton (15).

On the tour Yes will be supported by Jonathan Swift.

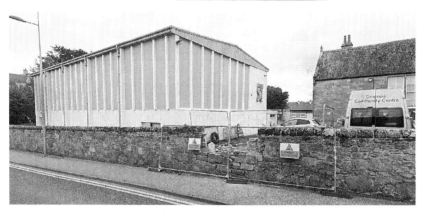

Thursday 29th July- Whiting bay, Isle Of Arran, Scotland
Also Top Of The Pops broadcast for 'Get Down And Get With It'.

Friday 30th July- Isle Of Arran, Scotland

Saturday 31st July- Isle Of Arran, Scotland

AUGUST 1971

Sunday 1st - Electric Gardens. Sauchiehall Street, Glasgow

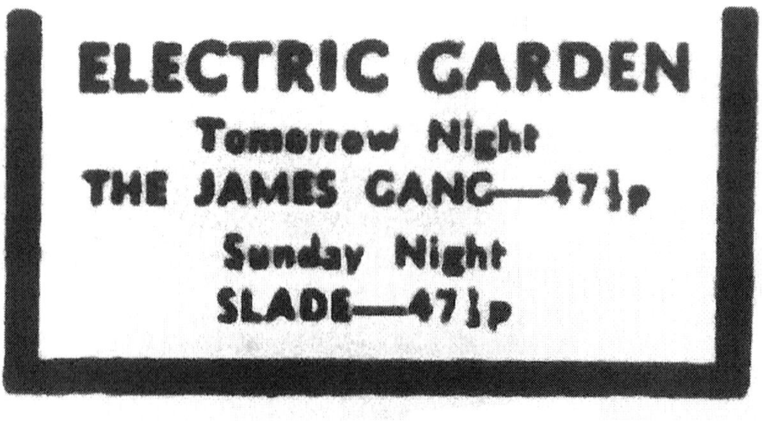

DO YER FING!
At the
OUTBACK
DISCO CLUB

The discotheque with the big sound
of the best discs around.
Open 9 p.m.-4 a.m. every Friday
and Saturday
105 BUCHANAN STREET
GLASGOW, C.2
Telephone: 041-332 4484

ELECTRIC GARDEN
Tomorrow Night
THE JAMES GANG—47½p
Sunday Night
SLADE—47½p

47 and a half pence. You can't get a bar of chocolate for that today.

58

Slade home dates — then Europe, U.S.

SLADE is set for dates in Scotland, Wales and England before commencing a European tour in mid-August. Manager Chas Chandler is currently negotiating a brief American visit for the group — and, if it materialises, Slade will fly to the States in late September or early October for ten days of promotion.

The outfit is at present engaged in a three-day stint at the Isle of Arran holiday resort, then it plays Glasgow Electric Garden (this Sunday) and Blackwood Institute (August 6) before travelling to Neath Gwyn Hall (7).

Slade returns to London to play Edmonton Cook's Ferry Inn (9), then goes back North to appear at Nairn Ballerina (11-16) doubling at Paisley Watermill (12), Ayr Bobby Jones Ballroom (13), Fife Burns Island Palms (14), Beardstone Kilmarnsey Stadium (15) and Dumfries Oughton's (16).

Thursday 5th
Top Of The Pops broadcast of video for 'Get Down And Get With It'.

Friday 6th - Blackwood Institute Pentwynd Road, Blackwood, Monmouthshire.

Another rather impressive and imposing Welsh building.

Saturday 7th - Gwyn Hall. Orchard Street, Neath.

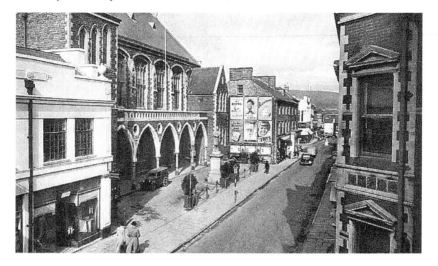

Monday 9th - Cooks Ferry Inn. Angel Road, Edmonton

Wednesday 11th - Ballerina Ballroom. High Street, Nairn, Scotland.

Thursday 12th - Watermill Hotel. Lonend, Paisley, Scotland.

THE
WATERMILL HOTEL
LONEND, PAISLEY

THURSDAY, 12th AUG.

PERSONAL APPEARANCE OF
THE SENSATIONAL

SLADE

(CURRENT RECORD IN
TOP TWENTY)

ALSO
THE REACTION DISCO

7.30-11 p.m.
Supper Tickets 50p
from Hotel Reception
(over 18's only)

THE WATERMILL
A REO STAKIS HOTEL

Friday 13th - Bobby Jones Pavilion. Burns Statue Square, Ayr, Scotland.

Saturday 14th - Palais Club Mantis Lane, Burntisland, Fife, Scotland.

Burntisland Palais.

Saturday 14th - TV - Whittakers World of Music
Also featuring Ginette Reno and J Vincent Edwards.

Also Saturday 14th : Disc and Music Echo feature:
'SLADE - OR WHEN THEIR HAIR FINALLY GREW'

"A year ago a lot of people back home walked on the other side of the street if they saw us coming so they didn't have to talk to us, says Dave Hill, never-ever serious lead guitarist of Slade. "But now with Get Down And Get With It in the chart, they come up to us in the street, shake out hands and say things like 'How you doing mate? Nice to see ya.' "

But that doesn't surprise Slade for they've never had it easy. They were launched three years ago on what seemed the perfect gimmick; they were announced as "the first skinhead group" at a time when boots and braces and shaven heads were the "in" thing. Yet somehow, they didn't take off as they should have. They were banned from halls by promoters afraid of riots, spurned by members of other groups, and suffered more knocks than any other group you could think of.

"People thought we were a put-together group," says lead singer Noddy holder, "and we became known as just a skinhead group. No one wanted to listen to our music. At first the knocks didn't bother us but when they went on and on, and the people knocking us were the people who hadn't bothered to listen to us, it got a bit much."

So how then did they finally manage to convince enough people of their talent to get their third single high in the chart? The answer is hard work and plenty of it. They've been working six, sometimes seven nights a week, gradually building a following by getting audiences raving wherever they've played.

Party nights

"Most nights it's like a party," says Noddy. "Instead of trying to educate the audience like a lot of groups do nowadays, we try to get them to feel part of what's going on. The visual aspect of the act is very important to us. In fact 50 per cent of the act is visual, the other 50 per cent concentrates on the music.

Their act has always been popular because of the atmosphere they create live. So they figured if they could get that feel on record they'd have a winner, So that's what they did with "Get Down And Get With It."

"We tried very much to get the excitement of the stage act on the record and I think we succeeded. That's why it was a hit. We could do it on stage and the kids could go away and buy it and get the same thing. That's what we want to try and do on the next album; not necessarily do rock and roll songs but get the same feel as the single."

But the single won't be a ballad either, "because we couldn't do much with that on stage. We feel we always have to be doing something on stage. Slow numbers we feel are real downers," says Noddy. "We like to keep raving, but we do a couple of slow things like

"Nights In White Satin" because we dare not leave them out now our audiences have got to know them. But if we do a slow number we have to fool around while we're doing it. We'll belch or something. We don't want to be pretentious and the slow things aren't us. We'd hate people to think we're preaching at them. We just want them to have a good time."

They emphasise though, that rockers they may be, but they also believe in melody. "At the moment," adds Noddy, "we're not as heavy as we want to be on record but we've got to think of the radio. We wouldn't get our records played if they were any heavier."

A live album by them is an obvious possibility. "But says bass guitarist Jimmy Lee (who complains they never show him on Top Of The Pops), "it would be a complete shambles. Completely chaotic. The kids get so involved ad leap about so much that leads would get broken and the sound wouldn't be all that good. But it might be an idea for us to do an album half live and half studio recorded."

Slade's main concern now when they get on stage is to create and atmosphere, to create excitement.

Says Dave: "It all started one night when we all got drunk and went on stage and had a good laugh. The kids all dug it and we enjoyed it. And that's the way it's been since. Not that we need to drink before we go on stage! But now we're a lot more confident. We've got to the stage now where we feel like if you don't like us you don't like us and it doesn't bother us."

Slade no longer dress like skinheads but their dress still attracts a lot of attention. They've gone from one extreme to the other. Now it's all bright colours, boots, dungarees and other such eye-brow-raising costumes. But that's all part of "showbiz."

Cheap group

That's what's got lost out of this business, " says Jimmy Lee, who's incidentally taken up playing the fiddle in the hope that it will bring him a few more camera shots. "All the flash has gone out of groups. You've got to give the audience something to think about. You've got to give them value for money."

"That's what the skinhead look was all about," says Noddy. "We were hoping to get the same effect, but we found a lot of people didn't dig that. As we look now we're getting over to more people. Before the people either liked it or they didn't. But we're not knocking it. It was something we did and tried and it was a laugh at the time. But now that we've broken through we're not going to outprice ourselves like so many groups do when they have a hit. Those that have been nice to us we'll play for at the usual price. But those that knocked us.... We're going to do them for every penny!"

Phil Symes

Sunday 15th - Kilnareinny Stadium. Kilnareinny Avenue, Beardstone.
This show is not confirmed to have taken place.
Projected headliners King Crimson played at Hyde Park, London on this date.

Monday 16th - Oughton's Rest. Church Place, Dumfries

This impressive building is now a toy shop on the ground level and
remains a live music venue as THE VENUE nightclub upstairs.

Thursday 19th - Top Of The Pops broadcast for 'Get Down And Get With It'.

Saturday 21st - Royal Links Pavillion. Overstrand Road, Cromer
Support: Barrabas

Sunday 22nd - Windsor Ballroom. Coaltham Hotel , Turner Street, Redcar

Friday 27th - Pavilion. The Esplanade, Weymouth, Dorset.

Monday 30th - Chelsea Village. Glen Fern Road Bournemouth.

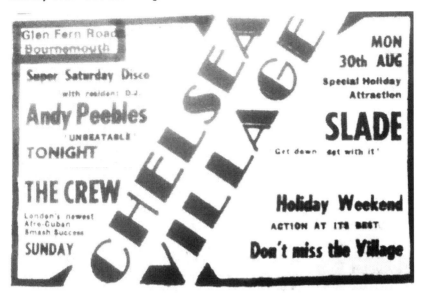

Andy Peebles spinning the discs.

Tuesday 31st - City Hall. Prince's Street, Truro, Cornwall.

SEPTEMBER 1971

Friday 3rd – The Top Rank. Silver Street, Doncaster.
Support: Station.

The Top Rank in Doncaster was part of a chain of venues that regularly hosted concerts by all of the greats of music. Doing better than some of the other venues that were in that same chain, which were either closed and then demolished, the Doncaster Top Rank would later continue to function as a music venue, firstly renamed as Visage and then later on as Rotters. Slade would return to the very same venue in 1980.

Saturday 4th - Kilmarenny Stadium, Beardstone.
Also on the bill: King Crimson - Lindisfarne - The Move. The actual line up at the show on this date remains unconfirmed, as King Crimson are known to have played a concert in Hyde Park, London on the date in question.

Sunday 5th – London. Benefit show in aid of Schizophrenia.
Also on the bill: Spike Milligan and many others.

Monday 6th - Cavendish. Berry Street, Wolverhampton

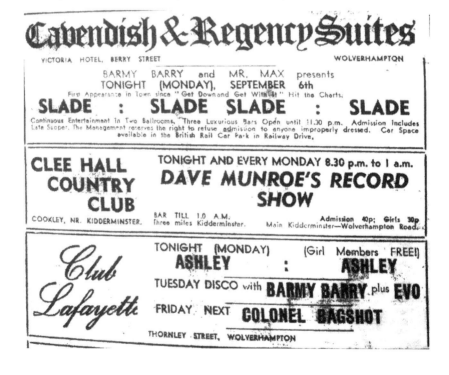

John Ogden reported on the London show from the 5th in the Wolverhampton Express And Star:

> *Only group in a concert on Sunday in aid of schizophrenics, in a top hotel in London, were Slade. And who else was on the bill? Spike Milligan, Peter Cook and Dudley Moore, and other top stars. The event was compered by Michael Caine, and Lord George Brown was in the audience. I gather he thought the group was rather loud.*
>
> *Next night was another one for showbiz, when many groups went to see Slade at Wolverhampton's Cavendish Suite. Naturally enough, they got a quitter reception than they usually do because it was a home town audience, but they still went down well and showed why they have become such a draw in most parts of the country.*

Wednesday 8th - Volunteer. High Street, Plumstead, Barking.

Saturday 11th - Town Hall. Magdalene Street, Glastonbury.

Wednesday 15th - Town Hall. The Headrow, Leeds.
Support: Brett Marvin and the Thunderbolts

JON PAUL PRESENTS AT

LEEDS TOWN HALL

WEDNESDAY, SEPT. 15th, at 7.30 p.m.

SLADE
BRETT MARVIN
& THE THUNDERBOLTS

Tickets: 80p, 70p, 65p, 60p, 50p & 40p

Available in advance from Track One, Grand Arcade, New Briggate, Leeds

Leeds Town Hall

jon paul PRESENTS

SOUTHEND 610152

September 12th
URIAH HEEP
Palace Theatre
Westcliff-on-Sea

September 15th
SLADE
+ MEDICINE HEAD
Town Hall
Leeds

October 17th
MEDICINE HEAD
+ BRETT MARVIN AND
THE THUNDERBOLTS
Palace Theatre
Westcliff-on-Sea

November 21st
GROUNDHOGS
+ SLOW HAND
Palace Theatre
Westcliff-on-Sea

December 4th
ATOMIC ROOSTER
+ CASTLE FARM
Kursaal
Southend-on-Sea

December 19th
WILD TURKEY
+ WRITING ON THE WALL
Palace Theatre
Westcliff-on-Sea

All bookings through STEVE BARNETT at BRON Agency
29-31 Oxford Street, London, W.1. Phone: 01-437 5063

Friday 17th - Training College. Folly Lane, Hereford

Saturday 18th - Marquee Club. Wardour Street, London

Monday 20th – Quaintways, Northgate Street, Chester -
Support: Danta

Then

Now. Quaintways is still functioning as a music venue (Rosie's) today.
On my rare forays into the North of England, Chester is the most gorgeous place I've seen.

A good month at Quaintways.

Friday 24th - Trocadero Ballroom, Hamilton, Scotland.
Support: Colour Blind.

Sunday 26th - Lamlash, Isle of Arran
Also on the bill: Nazareth / Thin Lizzie

Concert programme with Thin Lizzy (spelt correctly) named as the headline act.

Tuesday 28th - University, Cardiff

OCTOBER 1971

Friday 1st - Technical College, Huddersfield.
Support: Head Hands and Feet

Saturday 2nd - University, Hull

Tuesday 5th - Palais Club, Humberstone Gate, Leicester (private show)

Wednesday 6th - Derbyshire Yeoman. Ashbourne Road, Derby
Support: White Rabbit / Judas Priest

tonight

HAPPY

ONE

an evening of arts ball

with

SLADE

JUDAS PRIEST

WHITE RABBIT

at the

Derbyshire Yeoman

6tp.　　　8 p.m, · Late.
with headlights and discs

Thursday 7th - Llanelli Glen Ballroom, Wales
Support: Gipsy / Squidd.

Friday 8th - Chez. High Road, Leytonstone

On this date, Slade also announced that they were recording three live sessions at Command Studios, London in October for a possible live album. Admission would be free to those who applied to attend. Bargain.

SLADE: FREE SHOWS

SLADE is to perform three free concerts in London on October 19, 20 and 21. Venue will be the 330-seater Command Studios (101 Piccadilly), and the purpose of the concerts is to record sufficient material for the release of a Polydor live album at the end of the year. Says group manager Chas Chandler: "Anyone who wants to come along will be welcome." Sessions start at 8pm and last until about 11pm.

The outfit has been booked for an extensive schedule of one-nighters throughout this month. It visits Leytonstone Chez (tonight, Friday), Madeley College, Staffs (Saturday), Bolton Casino (next Monday), Cardiff Top Rank (Wednesday), Ayr Dam Park Hall (Thursday), Grennock Beau Brummel Club (October 15), Glasgow University (16), Dunfermline Kinema (17), Cuffley Youth Centre, Herts (22), Carmarthen St. Peter's Hall (23), Portsmouth Tricorn (25), Bristol Old Granary (26), Bournemouth Cardinal (27), Nottingham Palais (28), Birmingham Aston University (30) and Darwen Uncle Tom's Cabin (31).

Friday 8th - Coz I luv You / My Life Is Natural single released.

The song came about following Jim Lea going round to Noddy Holder's house one evening, carrying his wife's acoustic guitar. They had always messed about with a Django Reinhardt style jazz tune or two in their dressing room and while Jim was trying to come up with a new tune, he hit on the idea of making something out of the dressing room thing.

Some have said that it is similar in a way to Nine By Nine by the John Dummer Blues Band, but the similarity only really extends as far as the rhythm guitar style. The thumping walking bassline and the handclaps that they would later add would take the Slade song into a different league altogether. It's really quite a simple tune with a three chord verse and just a two chord chorus. Compared to their prog rock sound, this song was simplicity itself and it was a very catchy tune.

Their manager Chas Chandler told the group that he thought they had written their first number one.

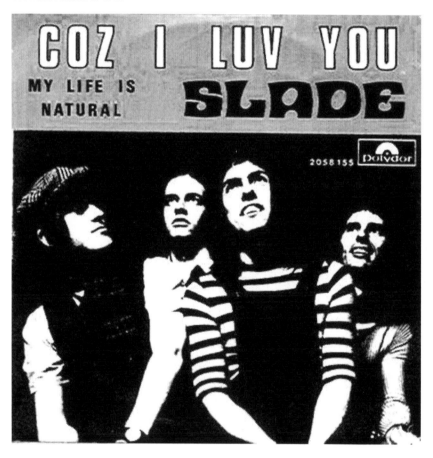

The group initially thought the song title 'Because I Love You' sounded 'a bit wet' and Jim Lea later said they thought the song itself was 'a bit wet too', so the title was changed to Coz I Luv You and the group beefed up the atmosphere of the backing track by stamping and clapping and whooping in the studio, to make it sound a lot more like a live recording.

Jim had been playing violin with the group in the studio and onstage and this was a good chance to show off his talents. The violin solo in the middle of the song was a unique sound for the pop charts at that time and the song soon caught on.

The group would continue to play Coz I Luv You onstage for the next year or so, with Jimmy Lea featured on violin and Dave Hill taking over on bass guitar duties for the song. Despite it being their first number one single, the group never really returned to playing it onstage in later years.

Saturday 9th - Madeley College, Staffordshire.

Also - Record Mirror article regarding Slade Alive! recording sessions.

SLADE FANS
OPEN HOUSE

THREE free concerts by Slade in London! That's the treat for the group's fans later this month when the four-piece go into the studios to record a 'live' album.

The 330-seat Command Recording Studios is the venue on October 19, 20 and 21 and, says group manager, Chas Chandler, "Anybody who wants to come along will be welcome. Not only will they get a free show, but they'll also have a unique opportunity of seeing the way that records are made these days."

The sessions start at 6p.m. each day and will last through until approximately 11p.m.

And the band's follow up single to their "Get Down And Get With It" hit, "Coz I Luv You", is released this Friday, which features a violin solo by lead guitarist Jimmy Lea, once a member of the Birmingham Youth Orchestra.

Greenwood adds two for dates

Monday 11th - Casino Club. Crompton Way, Bolton.

Support: DJ Paul Brett Sage. Slade only got a few numbers into their show before neighbour complaints obliged the venue management to call the show to a halt. The group repair back to the Pack Horse Hotel in Bolton. Did The Who encounter the same problems when they played there in April 1969?

91

The Casino Club in Bolton is now a Family Shopper outlet.

Wednesday 13th - Top Rank Club, Cardiff, Wales.

Slade's Scots dates

SLADE ARE in Scotland this week just prior to their recording session at London's Command Studios, which will be attended by fans. Dates are: (Oct 14) Dam Park Hall, Ayr; (15) Beau Brummel Club, Greenock; (17) Kinema Ballroom, Dunfermline.

Thursday 14th – Dam Park Hall. Content Avenue, Ayr, Scotland.

Friday 15th - Beau Brummel Club, Greenock, Scotland.

Saturday 16th - Queen Margaret Union. University Gardens, Glasgow, Scotland.

Sunday 17th - Kinema Ballroom. Pilmuir Street, Dunfermline, Scotland.

Friday saw Midge Ure playing with his early band Salvation.

Monday 18th - Locarno Club, Sunderland

Tuesday 19th - Command Studios, Piccadilly, London - Recording
Wednesday 20th - Command Studios, Piccadilly, London – Recording
Thursday 21st - Command Studios, Piccadilly, London – Recording
Also Top Of The Pops broadcast for 'Coz I Luv You'.

Derby ravers get Slade LP with-it

WITHOUT a contingent from Derby and District College of Art in the audience at the cutting of the first part of Slade's live album at Command Studios, Piccadilly, London, last week, I shudder to think what the record would have been like, writes RICHARD COX.

As usual, the music was great, but the London crowd who packed the small theatre /studio, where as much into it as I am into the reggae tune.

They just sat there and didn't seem to be in the slightest bit bothered about the fact that the idea of a live album was to have a "live" audience.

But, thanks to the Art College, who took a party down specially for the session (thanks for the lift lads), the recording was done amidst a mass of squirming, ravy bodies. And Slade loved it.

So we danced awhile, and leapt, and shouted, and stomped, and waved our arms, and generally generated enough atmosphere to get some of the liveliest of the rest of the crowd to their feet.

The band burst into a few ravers to get people excited, including Coz I Luv You, their current single which is better than their previous one, Get Down And Get With It, which they also played.

It was an hour-long set, packed full of goodies, witties and things, and a few name-checks. Cameras popped everywhere, and bassman Jimmy Lee burst a string, but all was all right and the faithful throng drifted out into the London night air (yeuk) with warm hearts and tired limbs.

Tremendous form

Slade were on tremendous form throughout and Don Powell coped well with the multitude of mikes that poked annoyingly at his drum kit.

Dave Hill (lead/rhythm/-vocals) was also on top form as he prodded his guitar at singer Noddy Holder, and the chick in yellow who was raving with the rest of us.

Manager Chas Chandler seemed well pleased with the evening.

Don't know when the LP comes out, but it is a must for anyone, as the publicity man, John Halsall, will doubtless tell everyone in due course,

Command
Studios

Sound recording

Command Studios Limited
201 Piccadilly, London W1V 9LE
Telephone 01-734 0181
Telex 288662

STUDIO ONE big enough for 80 musicians and 24 feet high—or an audience of 400 for "live" recording.

STUDIO TWO will hold 30 musicians

STUDIO THREE specially constructed "rock box" to give maximum separation

DISC CUTTING by Scully Westrex master lathe.

CONTROL ROOMS three identical, each with 24 x 24 boards with quadraphonic facility and recorders up to 16 tracks.

CCTV echo plates/chamber, copy/edit room, special parking facility

Command Studios was situated at 201 Piccadilly, London and was opened up in the autumn of 1970. It was formerly the BBC Studios and in the thirties 201 Piccadilly had been a Lyons restaurant where the trendy set of those times used to gather at tea dances. The BBC took the place over as the Stage Door Canteen, during the war years. It was used to broadcast troop shows. **Glenn Miller** is said to have made his last broadcast from there too and in the fifties it became known as Piccadilly One and the BBC used it for shows from the Dales to Saturday Club.

Friday 22nd - Youth Centre. Station Road, Cuffley, Hertfordshire.

Saturday 23rd - St Peters Hall. Nott Square, Camarthen, Wales.

Sunday 24th – Coz I Luv You at number 26 in the UK singles chart.

Monday 25th - Tricorn Club. Tricorn Centre, Charlotte Street, Portsmouth
Support: Thumper

Tuesday 26th - Granary Club. Queen Charlotte Street, Bristol.
Support: Fumble

Wednesday 27th - Cardinal Club. Glen Fern Road, Bournemouth.

Thursday 28th - Palais Club. Upper Parliament Street, Nottingham.
The Hollies / Slade / Warhorse / Dominic Behan.
Also Top Of The Pops broadcast for 'Coz I Luv You'.

Saturday 30th - University, Aston, Birmingham

Sunday 31st - Coz I Luv You at number 8 in the UK singles chart.

Sunday 31st - Uncle Tom's Cabin. School Street, Darwen, Lancashire.

138 CLUBS

UNCLE TOM'S
cabin
CABARET·CABARET·CABARET

UNBELIEVABLE ACTION
DOUBLE DISCO BLOW-UP
at the

BEACHCOMBER

SUNDAY 7.30 p.m. till MIDNIGHT
'Get down and get with it'
SLADE

Admission: Members 30p;
Guests 50p

Late Transport to Blackburn,
Burnley, Bolton, Accrington and
Preston.

NEXT WEEK
TAMMI LYNN

SCHOOL STREET, DARWEN
TEL.: 73930

NOVEMBER 1971

Monday 1st and week - BBC sessions broadcast on-Johnny Walker show.

Thursday 4th - Top Of The Pops broadcast for 'Coz I Luv You'.

Friday 5th - Christchurch College, Canterbury

The College main hall

Saturday 6th – Disc and Music Echo front cover feature:

'SLADE FIGHT AMERICAN HYPE TO STAY IN BRITAIN'

Slade, in the chart this week at No. 18 with 'Coz I Luv You,' fast follow-up to 'Get Down And Get With It' have turned down an offer to launch them in America as "the next Beatles" – in favour of consolidating their UK success.

A consortium of US businessmen in Britain talent-hunting saw Slade recording tie "live" LP recently, and a figure in excess of one million dollars was mentioned for the deal, involving a TV series filmed in the group's hometown Wolverhampton, a full length movie, and a heavily promoted States tour.

Group leader Noddy Holder explained: "The last thing we want to do is mess around the people who have put us where we are. Anyway, I'd rather break into the American scene naturally than with a big hype behind us."

Management spokesman John Steele added: "They'd be silly to go to the States now; no matter what the offer. They're just getting through to the British public. So many bands go to the US without any record success – it's a waste. We're certainly not going to see the fellows trundling about over there, burning up money and getting nowhere."

Slade's 'Get Down And Get With It' was not a hit in the States. Manager Chas Chandler flies out soon to organise promotion of 'Coz I Luv You'. Meanwhile the band visits France, Belgium and Holland for TV promotion on the first hit. The "live" LP will follow another single in the early spring.

Saturday 6th - Melody Rooms. Oak Street, Norwich

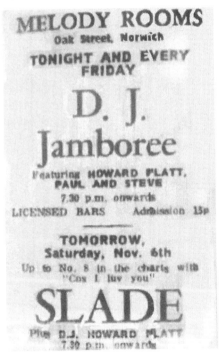

Sunday 7th – Coz I Luv You at number 1.

Thursday 11th - Memorial Hall. Gladstone Road, Barry, Wales
Also Top Of The Pops broadcast for 'Coz I Luv You'.

Saturday 13th – Slade are on the cover of the New Musical Express.

ROCK 'N' VIOLENCE

'It's not destructive – people just work out through the music.'

Suddenly it's rock and stomp time courtesy of Slade who with their two singles 'Get Down And Get With It' and 'Coz I Luv You' have injected some youthful exuberance into a rock scene almost sagging under the heavyweights but woefully short on new contenders for the main title.

Slade's only real major worry at this time is that their more immediate success on scene which takes its full toll of even the most talented new arrivals – remember Free, Taste and McGuinness Flint – should not dissipate overnight and that they convince their audience there is more in their music than meets the eye.

There are a number of very good reasons why this band should not fade in the preliminaries, not the least of which is their undoubted unity and the ability of musicians like bass/violinist Jimmy Lea and the aggressive vocal attack of guitarist/vocalist Noddy Holder.

Nod is a very different kettle of rock from most of the over-earnest new brigade of musicians anxious to prove that they can outplay the Stones, Zeppelin or the Who overnight. He was brought up on a steady diet of Everly Brothers at an early age when he bought his first single 'Cathy's Clown' out of his own pocket money but the crunch came one night in Wolverhampton listening to the early Spencer Davis Group.

"They were almost underground in those days," recalled nod with a grin. "Anyway they came on stage to applause instead of screams which I remember was very unusual in those days. Then they opened very quietly with Spencer and Muff playing softly.

"Half way through the number, just as I was beginning to ask myself what the big deal was all about, this spotty kid on the organ opened his mouth and screamed 'AH JUST LOVE THE WAY SHE WALKS' and I sat there with my face hanging out. I thought that voices like that only came out of Georgia and the band went on to rock like mad. I just had to get myself into a group who played that loud and that good."

So you can safely say that Nod has never been the same man since that traumatic experience with Messrs Winwood and Co and if you listen to the hard edge on his vocals it's not difficult to realise the soulful quality springs from the same sort of early R&B background as Stevie.

He believes that Slade's strength and sustaining power lies in its' 'stickability.'

"I've never been a great fan of the super-guitarists like Clapton, Gallagher or Lee," said Nod. "The groups that have made the greatest contribution to rock music are those like The Who who have stuck it out and built up something which was bigger than any one individual. I think we are beginning to do that – it only really comes about by sticking it out through the hard times."

Slade's early spawning ground was the rather exotic area of the Bahamas where they played for almost six months to work off a hotel bill which they had been conned with in their embryonic state as the In-Betweens.

"They booked us into the best hotel on the island – people like Sean Connery stayed there. We thought great – nice of 'em to fix us up and pay for it – then they sold the pace and left us in the lurch. The only way we could pay for the hotel was to move out fast into a hovel and work it off."

"In a way it helped us more than anything because once you have to put up with each other for six months living in the same room you have a fair idea about your compatibility. We played everything during that period from Limbo to Moby Grape. It gave us a real musical understanding to build on."

Nod still cherishes some memorable gems from the early days in Wolverhampton when he used to give Robert Plant and his group Listen a lift in his father's window cleaning van during the period when they had no transport.

"I remember we played one gig supporting Cream at the City Hall and 'Plantey' was on the same bill as well. Even in those days he liked to move about the stage a bit but after Ginger Baker had set up his battery of drums he had no chance. He took his life in his hands and asked Ginger if he would mind moving his drums so he had a bit of space!"

Mr Baker is alleged to have requested Mr. Plant to vacate the immediate vicinity – or words to that effect.

You only have to see Slade onstage these days to realise that the group has something a bit extra to give from the usual new bands – they have a 'to hell with it all' attitude and good humoured aggression which is contagious. It's a good time band with the emphasis on getting everyone to enjoy and participate in the proceedings.

"We don't want rows of inanimate blobs sitting there trying to read some sort of psychological motivation into what we are doing – what we are doing si rocking – and we *want people up off their backsides and enjoying it as much as we are. We reckon if there's anyone left sitting down after we've finished that it's been a bad night."*

There is a sort of violence associated with our music but it's not a destructive type – people work out through the music. Young people have a lot of energy and we just help some of 'em get it on and work out."

Keith Altham

RECORD MIRROR article written by Bill McAllister:

Backstage, about half an hour before he struck the first chord in earnest, Slade's Dave Hill said, "If this live album works then it will set a pattern for us and we'll probably repeat it.

"We're trying to discover something for ourselves. We want to know what is right for us as a group. We'll soon know.

Probably by now Slade do know within themselves whether their experiment – the recording of their next album 'live' before a few hundred people at London's Command recording studios – has worked. We will have to wait until around Christmas time, maybe until New Year.

At a time when their single, 'Coz I Luv You' is careering up RM's charts their main concern is for the album. It tears, I think into their conscience. You can almost feel the exasperation there, a tight, desperate need to achieve something bigger than hit singles. It's an old drive, one that has affected many artists since the rise of contemporary rock music to 'art' level, born with the conception of 'Sgt. Pepper'.

There's no need, of course, to talk about Slade's music on 'art' levels, for it is nothing more or less than funky, well-played rock, today's music. The album merely represents a fullness of ideas, not the presentation of a lifestyle or philosophy. Slade's main concern, from what I understand of their music, is to gain recognition – and thus popularity – for the music as well as the image.

The image, as we know too well, was there first. The skinhead look that backfired on them – aggression creates aggression – has only now subsided. Slade are a hard-working band, playing mainly in the provinces and the still all too uncharted regions of Scotland and Wales, for fans more than eager in their starved anticipation for exciting, raw music. And faithful in their devotion, too, having established the band firmly in the singles charts.

"Then the fans come up and ask us if we have an album out. And it's a bit sad that there is only 'Play It Loud' because it is so dated. We should have recorded a live album ages ago." Dave Hill looks at drummer Don Powell and they both nod resigned agreement.

The first night was 'just a trial.' But enough good material was expected over the three nights to make up an extremely palatable album, representative of Slade in every way.

If you're a determined Slade fan you'll rejoice to know that versions of 'Knights In White Satin', 'Darlin' Be Home Soon' and Hear Me Callin'' will be included. And Steppenwolf's 'Born to Be Wild', number much-requested.

"We've tried to drop it from the act several times," says Don in his opening gambit, "but the crowds always shout for it."

"At one time," chips in Dave, "we were going to record it as a single and then the Steppenwolf version came out here."

Later in the evening, before a somewhat unmoved audience, seemingly too scared to vent emotions for fear of disrupting the sessions, Slade went through their paces and dutifully produced a very, very loud interpretation of 'Born To Be Wild'. True to their word it was uninhibited in frenzied spirit as anyone could have wished for. "We won't go on thinking that we've got to get it down straight off," Dave said. "We've got time to play with."

However, it is not only a crucial time for Slade as regards recording, since it becomes increasingly apparent that in 'live' appearances they have yet to break out of the 'club' circuit into concerts, a realm generally considered much more suited to intelligent musical appreciation.

Slade are adamant, though, that they will stay in clubs for as long as it feels right. "It would be a bit too adventurous," says Hill with a shake of his head, "to do anything like an Albert Hall concert at the moment."

"The group's fans," manager Chas Chandler interposes, "could fill the Albert Hall twice over if we wanted it like that. We don't need it."

"We could do it, though," Hill comes back, "if we were supporting an act like The Who. Gigs are best for us when they have an atmosphere. A warmth."

Saturday 13th - The Roundhouse. Lodge Avenue, Dagenham, Essex.

Sunday 14th - Blades Club (Black Prince). Southwold Road, Bexley, Kent

BLACK   PRINCE   HOTEL,
BEXLEY, KENT

SLADE

BUMPERS
VELVET UNDERGROUND

The Black Prince at Bexley

Sunday 14th - Coz I Luv You at number 1.

Tuesday 16th - Starlight Rooms. Spain Place, Boston, Lincolnshire.

A change of name in later years...

Wednesday 17th - Top Rank. Park Lane, Sunderland
Support: Good Habit

What was once a Top Rank is now a Blue Monkey.

Thursday 18th - Locarno Club. Newcastle Road Sunderland.
Also Top Of The Pops broadcast for 'Coz I Luv You'.

Friday 19th - College Of Education, Birmingham.

Saturday 20th - Starlight Ballroom. Spain Place, Boston, Lincolnshire.
Support: McKendree Spring

Sunday 21st - Excel Bowl. Caversham Road, Middlesborough.

Monday 22nd and week - BBC sessions broadcast on Johnny Walker show.

Wednesday 24th - Town Hall. Wakefield Old Road, Dewsbury, Yorkshire.

Thursday 25th - Top Of The Pops broadcast for 'Coz I Luv You'.

Friday 26th - Trocadero Ballroom. Townhead Street, Hamilton

Saturday 27th - Embark on Short European Tour for TV

Sunday 28th - Coz I Luv You at number 1.

Sunday 28th – Travel to Belgium.
Monday 29th - Pop Deux Studio Brussels, Belgium, recording 'PopShop'
Tuesday 30th – Europe TV.

DECEMBER 1971

Wednesday 1st – Europe

■ Week ending 4 Dec 1971

▶1	1	Coz I Luv You SLADE *Polydor*		6
2	3	Ernie (The Fastest Milkman In The West) BENNY HILL *Columbia*		4
3	2	Jeepster T. REX *Fly*		4
▶4	4	Gypsys, Tramps And Thieves CHER *MCA*		5
5	5	Johnny Reggae PIGLETS *Bell*		5
6	14	Tokoloshe Man JOHN KONGOS *Fly*		3
7	8	Banks Of The Ohio OLIVIA NEWTON-JOHN *Pye International*		6
8	6	Till TOM JONES *Decca*		7
9	7	I Will Return SPRINGWATER *Polydor*		7
▶10	12	Run, Baby, Run (Back Into My Arms) NEWBEATS *London*		6
11	21	Something Tells Me (Something Is Gonna Happen Tonight) CILLA BLACK *Parlophone*		3
12	10	Surrender DIANA ROSS *Tamla Motown*		5
▶13	18	Sing A Song Of Freedom CLIFF RICHARD *Columbia*		3
14	9	Maggie May ROD STEWART *Mercury*		12
15	–	No Matter How I Try GILBERT O'SULLIVAN *Mam*		1
16	–	Theme From 'Shaft' ISAAC HAYES ✱ *Stax*		1
17	23	For All We Know SHIRLEY BASSEY *United Artists*		16
18	15	The Night They Drove Old Dixie Down JOAN BAEZ *Vanguard*		9
19	13	Look Around (And You'll Find Me There) VINCE HILL *Columbia*		9
20	19	Let's See Action WHO *Track*		5
21	32	Fireball DEEP PURPLE *Harvest*		3
▶22	30	Riders On The Storm DOORS *Elektra*		5
23	11	Tired Of Being Alone AL GREEN *London*		9
24	16	The Witch Queen Of New Orleans REDBONE *Epic*		10
25	38	Is This The Way To Amarillo TONY CHRISTIE *MCA*		2
26	36	Hooked On A Feeling JONATHAN KING *Decca*		2
27	–	It Must Be Love LABI SIFFRE ✱ *Pye International*		1
28	–	Softly Whispering I Love You CONGREGATION ✱ *Columbia*		1
29	34	You Gotta Have Love In Your Heart SUPREMES AND THE FOUR TOPS *Tamla Motown*		
30	25	Chinatown MOVE *Harvest*		

115

Thursday 2nd - - Top Of The Pops broadcast for 'Coz I Luv You'.

Friday 3rd - Ranmore complex Students Union, Sheffield University

Friday 4th - Mardi Gras Club. Mount Pleasant Street, Liverpool.

Thank you to all the people who produced such good vibes at our first progressive Saturday concert. We hope to see you all this week to see the Number 1 group, who were 1970's top college group AT THE MARDI GRAS CLUB, SATURDAY, DECEMBER 4.

SLADE

On stage 11 p.m., plus Wave, plus Light Show, Record Shop, 50p

Friday 4th - Padgate College, Warrington.

SOUND 71

Slade's long cut to fame!

by DAVID WIGG

WHEN SLADE changed from "skinheads" into "hairies" they changed their luck.

Today, with long hair, these four lads from the Black Country are the latest teenage rage of Britain.

Hysteria breaks out at their stage appearances, and their No. 1 record " Coz

NODDY BEFORE

NODDY AFTER

The Slade's lead singer, Noddy Holder, says the skinhead image backfired on them.

I Luv You " sold as many as 250,000 in the first week of release.

This week it has broken into the U.S. charts.

But, as experience shows, all this has happened to several pop groups in the past —most of whom have since drifted into oblivion.

Slade have not given any thought to their success burning out.

"It's been a hard slog all the way. It's not overnight success as far as we are concerned," said their lead singer, 21-year-old Noddy Holder, in a thick Midland accent. "We have been on the road professionally as we are now for about three years.

"That's where we built up our following. The hit records have come at a great time, but the mainstay of our following are young people who have seen us on stage.

"We feel our backbone is the hard core of fans who would stay by us even if we didn't have any success with records."

The son of a Wolverhampton window cleaner, Noddy—it's a nickname from his Comprehensive school days where he gained six G.C.E. "O" levels —explained why the group decided to rid themselves of their skinhead image.

Trouble

" It really backfired on us," he said. " Skinheads started getting bad publicity and so promoters stopped booking us, because they thought we would attract trouble. So we decided we would have to grow our hair. But we still continue to play the same kind of music."

Noddy has a girl friend back in Wolverhampton, but says: " She knows what I'm like on the road—so she doesn't take me seriously.

Slade have been promoted into the big time by ex-Animal group member Chas Chandler.

The three other members of Slade are drummer Don Power, lead guitarist Dave Hill, and bass player Jimmy Lea.

Slade, who have just returned from an extensive tour of the Continent, are now working on a "live" LP.

DISC

STAY WITH ME (The Faces, Warner K16136). This song by Ronnie Wood and Rod Stewart has a most beguiling message —" Stay with me tonight but tomorrow I'll kick you out." Their rock 'n' roll rave-up playing makes the harsh message less offensive.

JUDITH SIMONS.

Wednesday 9th - Tower Ballroom. Marine Parade, Great Yarmouth, Norfolk

Thursday 10th - Polytechnic, Leeds

Friday 11th - Technical College, Watford, Hertfordshire
Support: Supertramp / Good Habit

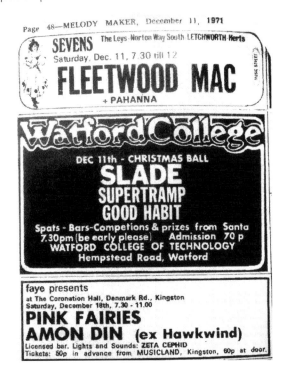

Wednesday 15th - Floral Hall. The Promenade, Southport
Support: Jimmy McCullough Band / Little Free Rock

SOUTHPORT FLORAL HALL
Wednesday, 15th December

SLADE

plus **JIMMY McCULLOCH BAND**
LITTLE FREE ROCK

Tickets 70p (adv.), 75p door

K.C.F.E. PRESENTS AT
CORONATION HALL, KINGSTON, SURREY
(Penrhyn Road)
SATURDAY, 11th DECEMBER

AMERICA (from U.S.A.)

MAN + + WALRUS
DISCO ● LIGHTS ● BAR
Admission: 50p S.U. (cards) and in advance from
Musicland, Kingston, or S.U. Offices (Poly and
K.C.F.E.). 60p at the door
Special guest of the evening **JEFF DEXTER**

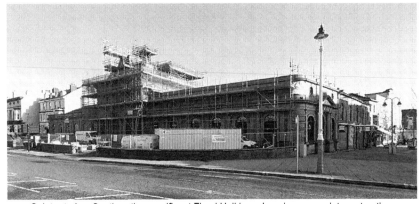

Quieter today: Southport's magnificent Floral Hall is undergoing a complete restoration.
It is going to reopen as a venue despite the owners, Bliss, going bankrupt during the pandemic
and turning the properties over to the Council, who are currently redeveloping the building.

Thursday 16th - South College, Bristol (Christmas Lost World Ball)
Support: Squid / Pigsty Hill.

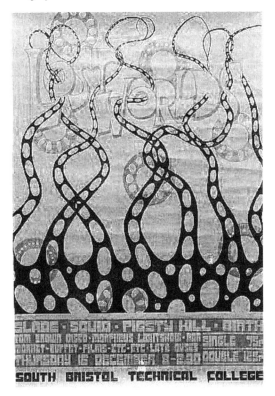

Friday 17th - College, Slough, Berkshire
Support: Queenie / Gnidrolog.

Saturday 18th - Alex Discotheque, Salisbury, Wiltshire.

ALEX DISCO
SALISBURY

THIS SATURDAY, 18th DECEMBER

"Christmas Coupe" — Special engagement of

 ★ **SLADE** ★

Members 40p   Dancing...8 to 11.45 p.m.   Visitors 50p

YOUR D.J. DISCOMOBILE

Monday 20th - Town Hall. Wakefield Old Road, Dewsbury, Yorkshire
Support: Mosaic

DEWSBURY TOWN HALL

DEWSBURY PARISH YOUTH CLUB presents
hit recorders of COZ I LUV YOU ——

SLADE

Plus MOSAIC and ——
STEVE JAMES DISCO

MONDAY, 20th DECEMBER, 1971.

Tickets 50p :: 7-30 'til late :: Adm. at door 60p

Tickets from Rawlinsons Travel Agency,
Westgate, Dewsbury.

Tuesday 21st - Public Hall. Fleet Street, Preston, Lancashire

Thursday 23rd - Up The Junction. South Street, Crewe

One sometimes wonders if the owners of these previous venues knew what went before?

Friday 24th - Marquee Club. Wardour Street, London

Monday 27th – repeat Top Of The Pops broadcast for 'Coz I Luv You'.

Wednesday 29th - The Boathouse. Kew Bridge, Kew.

The December fan club newsletter thanked fans for their support and also mentioned that fans should look out for their new album Slade Alive. The Sun had run a competition to design a cover for the record. A punishing schedule was set for January and February of the next year.

And what else would 1972 bring?

BIBLIOGRAPHY AND THANKS

FEEL THE NOIZE.
Chris Charlesworth. Omnibus.

LOOK WOT I DUN
Lise Lyng Falkenberg. Omnibus.

WHO'S CRAZEE NOW?
Noddy Holder / Lisa Verrico. Ebury.

THE WORLD ACCORDING TO NODDY HOLDER.
Noddy Holder. Constable.

SLADE
George Tremlett. Futura.

THE SLADE PAPERS
Music Sales Ltd.

BRAVO SCRAPBOOK
Rexpert Books.

CUM ON FEEL THE NOIZE
Alan G Parker and Steve Grantley

THE NOIZE Second Edition.
Chris Selby / Ian Edmundson.
Self-publish. Amazon.

SIX YEARS ON THE ROAD
Ian Edmundson. Self-publish, Amazon.

SLADE IN FLAME
John Pigeon. Panther.

SO HERE IT IS.
Dave Hill. Unbound.

There are a number of people who I would like to thank.

Thanks to:

The members of Slade.

The Slade book writers. There are some great new books out there.

The Slade website people.

The people who actually answered my emails and messages.

All the people who ran Slade Fan Club magazines.

Nigel, Dee, Davey and Bernie for advice.

Yes, other interesting bands were playing on the same nights, so I have shown a few of those too, rather than losing those adverts.

I'm a fan, sometimes a short story writer, and I felt that Slade deserved another book or two. Thanks to the people who offered some self-publishing advice. It's not that easy to get a book out there, so it was very much appreciated.

Thanks for looking at this book, which is totally unofficial.

Love to Lisa.

Printed in Great Britain
by Amazon

84546604R00072